MW01608049

PASSAGES

HOW READING THE BIBLE
IN A YEAR WILL CHANGE
EVERYTHING FOR YOU

STUDY GUIDE

BRIAN HARDIN

WINDFARM BOOKS
A DIV. OF DAILY AUDIO BIBLE

WindFarm

Passages Study Guide
©2012 Brian Hardin

ISBN 978-0-9882583-0-3

The original Passages: How Reading The Bible In A Year is available from Zondervan
in paperback, eBook and Audio Edition wherever books are sold.

Published in the United States of America.

CONTENTS

I wrote Passages : How Reading The Bible In A Year Will Change Everything For You for one reason although it took some time to figure that out. When I was approached about writing this book it was unbelievably intimidating. What more can be said about the Bible? How many more thousands of pages of commentary can there possibly be? What do I have to say that hasn't already been said better? And who has the audacity to write about God's Word itself anyway?

But the more time and contemplation that I put into the task the more I realized that something was missing from the libraries of solid advice and deep theological concepts we use to formulate our convictions about the Christian faith. I'd tried to read the Bible and came to the same conclusions that so many do. That it's hard to understand. That it's cryptic. That it's customs are so far removed from modern society that it's hard to even know what God was trying to say in the first place. That I don't have time to become a theologian to unleash its power. On and on.

When I started reading the Daily Audio Bible I came to Scripture from a place I'd never been before. I stared at the dusty old book and asked it if it could actually speak to me and if it did would it be God's voice that I heard back. I came honestly. I came without assumptions. I needed to know. The weak faith that was my normal life was at an end. I needed God to speak and I didn't know where I was supposed to go other than to this dusty book.

And God came for me. As the days turned to weeks and months He came for me in the most surprising ways and by the time I'd reached the last word of the last Chapter of the Bible I'd changed altogether but so had the Bible (or at least my perception of it.)

What I'd never heard anyone tell me before was that the Bible isn't a rule book that I needed to measure my sorry self against. Sure, I'd heard it was a manual for life or that it was **B**-asic **I**-nstructions **B**-efore **L**-eaving **E**-arth but honestly that all felt lame and weak to my actual living, breathing life. Nobody told me that the Bible would become the best friend I'd never had.

As the days and prayers and long nights on my back patio forged ahead I began to write with the hope that I could somehow re-frame the Bible. To take away the misconceptions and misrepresentations and replace them with a compelling enough reason for people to try again.

Of course writing a book about the Bible an a way that encompasses all it's mysteries and wisdom is impossible. This is why millions of pages have been written over thousands of years about it. But that's not what Passages is about. Passages is an honest look at why you should read the Bible written from a very honest place and it's a truthful look at what you can expect if you take the leap and dive in.

This study guide is intended to help a person or a small group work through the Passages book. But if all that happens is that Passages becomes another "Bible study," or "Small Group Resource," I'll be disappointed. *DO* make it both of those things but at the end of your study I hope more than anything that a smoldering desire was stoked into a spark that gives you the desire to take the greatest adventure of your life into the epic love story between the sovereign God and His people. You are one of those people and this story is not over. You have a role to play in it and I pray you find your place because you are needed now more than ever.

HOW TO USE THIS STUDY GUIDE

This study guide assumes that you or a group of you are using Passages: How Reading The Bible In A Year Will Change Everything For You as the center of your study time or book club reading. So to overstate the obvious, you need to read the book.

The material in this study guide are laid out by chapter. There are ten chapters in Passages. Read a chapter of the book then reflect. If you're doing this in a group it's a great ten part series of discussions that will ask you to reflect on your relationship with God and His Word.

Each section contains a summary of the chapter and provides discussion questions followed by a reaction or reflection point that challenges you to do something tangible with the time you've spent discussing things. Each time you meet you should begin by checking in with each other about how you've put your discussion to good use in your life.

It probably also goes without saying that the Daily Audio Bible is available to you free of charge every single day in any number of ways. You can go to www.dailyaudiobible.com and learn more about the Daily Audio Bible community and listen from there, you can go to any website or app that will receive a podcast and search for "Daily Audio Bible" and it should pop right up. iTunes is the most robust and significant collection of podcasts and it will allow you to download the DAB every day. The Daily Audio Bible also has apps for your Apple and Android devices. You can find these right from your phone and the app will give you the DAB every day wherever you are. You can also go to biblegateway.com and click "Bible Reading Plans." The Daily Audio Bible is there and you can listen and follow along from the text and translation we're reading from that week.

CHAPTER ONE
The Olive Couch

Read chapter one.

SUMMARY:

The previous year had started like the rest: work hard and then work hard to get more hard work. I'd tossed a New Year's prayer earnestly enough to God, the one about wanting to get closer to him and read the Bible more, but I had all but forgotten it by the second week of January.

By the end of the year I found myself sitting alone on my couch, devastated. The kingdom of work I'd built had crumbled before my eyes in a matter of months, and now I was in a crisis of faith. I vividly remember the prayer I prayed then. It wasn't a sinner's prayer, and it wasn't eloquent.

"Jesus, I'm done with the crap. I'm finished. If you want me to go to Des Moines and make hamburgers for a living, I'll pack up our stuff tomorrow and leave. I'm fine with that," I prayed. "I'm going to believe that you're nearby and that you can seize me before I hit the bottom. If you don't, I'm dead. I believe my heart will die, and I fear it will be the last time I care about anything."

God showed up for me that night, and began to whisper truth into my life. And then one night I received a bona fide directive from the Lord, an instruction to do something I would never, ever have done on my own: "I want you to podcast the Bible."

Earlier that year I had started to read the Bible every day. My friend Brad and I were traveling so much for work that I had gotten into the habit of reading it aloud to him in the car. I wasn't reading the Bible to gain deep insights into the mystical regions of the soul or to solve theological quandaries. I was just reading it for what it said, and often it said something that got stuck in a corner of my mind and loitered there for days. Stuff like, "The person who plants selfishness, ignoring the needs of others—ignoring God!—harvests a crop of weeds. All he'll have to show for his life is weeds! But the one who plants in response to God, letting God's Spirit do the growth work in him, harvests a crop of real life, eternal life" (Galatians 6:7 – 8 MSG). This was my life right there on the page, echoing prophetically over a couple millennia. It not only contextualized what I'd been experiencing; it gave me a north star and a measure of hope that I couldn't rationalize but I couldn't deny either.

So I obeyed God's direction and began to read a portion of the Bible every day. When I completed my first full revolution through the Bible, I recall looking in the mirror and realizing that I didn't see anything the same. I had been unwittingly transformed from the inside out, and I looked at just about everything through different eyes.

My friendship with the Bible has taken me the scenic route from who I was to who I was created to be. My path began with an act of obedience to read the Bible every day, and it wound its way almost backward to the beginning, forcing me to deal with the stresses and compulsions of trying to carve out an identity that was mine alone with God relegated to a back-up plan. It took me back to the wounds that life can bring and invited me to compare what they were saying about me with what God was declaring over me.

It can do the same for you.

Discussion Questions:

1. In Chapter One Brian shares his personal story of how he fell in love with the Bible. Share a little bit of your personal journey of faith with the group. What role has the Bible played in your story?

2. What has been your relationship with the Bible? How have you interacted with it in the past?

3. Brian says, "The previous year had started like the rest: work hard and then work hard to get more hard work. I'd tossed a New Year's prayer earnestly enough to God, the one about wanting to get closer to him and read the Bible more, but I had all but forgotten it by the second week of January.' How many times has reading the Bible been a New Year's resolution for you? How far did you get? If you stopped at some point what caused you to lose interest or allow that New Year's passion to fade?

4. In Brian's personal story he says, "My friendship with the Bible has taken me the scenic route from who I was to who I was created to be. My path began with an act of obedience to read the Bible every day, and it wound its way almost backward to the beginning, forcing me to deal with the stresses and compulsions of trying to carve out an identity that was mine alone with God relegated to a back-up plan. It took me back to the wounds that life can bring and invited me to compare what they were saying about me with what God was declaring over me. "

5. What would you hope the Bible would do for you?

Reflection:

What challenged you in this chapter?

What will you do now? Based on today's discussion how specifically are you going to live this out this week?

Who will you tell? With whom will you have a spiritual conversation with about this weeks discussion?

Notes:

_____

_____

_____

_____

_____

_____

_____

_____

_____

_____

_____

_____

_____

_____

_____

_____

_____

_____

_____

_____

_____

_____

CHAPTER TWO
Why Don't We Read The Bible

Read chapter two.

Summary:

I believe the Bible is the very Word of God, and that what we need for the life we were created to live is contained within its chambers. This Word is a lamp to our feet, and in the dark it will light our path (Psalm 119:105). In the gospel of Matthew, Jesus tells a story: "The kingdom of heaven is like treasure hidden in a field. When a man found it, he hid it again, and then in his joy went and sold all he had and bought that field" (Matthew 13:44). This is the reality of the Bible. It offers us a complete change of paradigm that leads to authentic freedom.

Surveys have shown that most people believe the Bible is the truth and that it holds the answer to the basic questions of life, and yet few of us spend any extended time in Bible study. Even though we claim to need it, we seem to avoid it. Where is the disconnect? Why don't we read the Bible if we believe it is God's Word and contains the answers to life's questions?

There are the obvious distractions. There is no shortage of excuses. But how could something so important seem to mean so little? The ironies compound themselves because we want to have a better relationship with God, we believe the Bible is the truth, and we believe it contains answers for our lives, yet reading the Bible is the one thing we continue to ignore.

There's a sobering reality lurking just beneath the surface, one we probably wouldn't say out loud: maybe we don't really believe reading the Bible will work for us. Maybe it will work for really spiritual people like pastors and missionaries, but not for us. The problem is that this line of thinking makes confetti of the faith we thought we had.

But maybe it's time. Maybe unraveling the layers of life and what we thought we believed will lead us to what we've been searching for all along: the truth, a foundation, a holy context for life.

It's time to abandon the limitations we've placed on the Bible. The Bible is written as a story, a story that has not yet reached its conclusion. The story has wound its way through battlefields and wedding nights, through birthing chambers and funeral parlors, from transcendent pleasure to utter hopelessness. The story has come through voices around Bedouin campfires to stone tablets, from the skins of animals to the printing press. It has passed through ages long forgotten to ages dark and forgettable. Its echoes bound from enlightenments to reformations. This is the unstoppable story of God and his profound love for humanity.

You are a part of this story. Your ancestors and heroes are contained within these pages. This is your story. To become intimate with the Bible is to finally find yourself. To understand that the stage is set and you have a role to play in God's story is finally to come home. Once you do, you will begin to see with the eyes of your heart, the way you were meant to.

Discussion Questions:

1. Most people would agree that the Bible is God's Word and contains truth. Most would also agree that the Bible contains God's plan for the restoration and salvation of mankind. Would you agree with that?

2. Ironically most people who would agree to these statements also do not regularly read the Bible. What are the things that interfere with a daily interaction with Scripture?

3. How important is a relationship with the Bible to a relationship with God? Why?

4. Do you think you need to be a religious or very spiritual person to understand the Bible or for God to speak through it?

5. Have you ever thought of the Bible as a story?

6. Have you considered that this story continues and you have a role to play God's story? If so, how has that changed the way you live day-to-day? If not, what does the idea that the Bible is your story bring up in your heart?

Reflection:

What challenged you in this chapter?

What will you do now? Based on today's discussion how specifically are you going to live this out this week?

Who will you tell? With whom will you have a spiritual conversation with about this weeks discussion?

Notes:

_____

_____

_____

_____

_____

_____

_____

_____

_____

_____

_____

_____

_____

_____

_____

_____

_____

_____

_____

_____

_____

CHAPTER THREE
The Benefits And Blessings Of Reading Scripture

Read chapter three.

Summary:

So what's supposed to happen if we read the Bible every day? What can we really expect?

I can say with all honesty that everything will change — but it may not be the way that you'd think. Change will happen from the inside out, not the outside in. If you're looking for a genie in a bottle, you will be disappointed. The Bible isn't a magic book of ancient wisdom; it's a book about life and about God's love for you.

In John 15 Jesus uses the metaphor that he is the vine and we are the branches. He breaks it down in simple terms by telling us that life is not going to work apart from him. If we remain in him, he will remain in us, and that connection will bring life. There is no possibility of true life outside of this connection, for without him we can do nothing.

A branch gets its nourishment from the vine or trunk. Our spiritual nourishment comes from Scripture, which provides the context for a dynamic relationship with God. This isn't just religious jargon thrown in for encouragement. Our relationship with God is informed by Scripture, and according to Jesus this relationship is what gives us life itself.

We are all seeking life. It's built into our DNA. Every commercial offers it and every romance novel, every magazine article, and every toy we buy promises to give it to us. Sometimes we settle for counterfeits such as materialism, an addiction, or any other obsession; but in the end, everything fails to give us what we want. The entire book of Ecclesiastes is a study on the meaninglessness of life without God, written from the perspective of a man who had seen and done it all. King Solomon had over a thousand of the world's most beautiful women waiting for his call. He had riches and honor that brought dignitaries from far and wide just to observe it; his wisdom and cunning were feared and revered. From an earthly perspective, his exploits are still referred to thousands of years later. Yet, in the end, he found it to be meaningless. All of his pleasures and pursuits did not bring life. What Solomon sought — and what we all seek — is authentic life. Jesus said, "The thief comes only to steal and kill and destroy; I have come that they may have life, and have it to the full" (John 10:10). Full and abundant life, Jesus says, is the very reason he came. This life cannot be found in earthly pursuits alone. King Solomon, the wisest man ever known, demonstrates this. Jesus, God in flesh, demonstrates this.

When we expect external things to bring us peace and happiness, we live our lives backward — outside in rather than inside out. Living from the inside out correctly orients us to the vine, the life force of God within us. From this place of connectedness we experience the abundance we crave. And when we have an insatiable desire for more of God, we are truly living an authentic life.

Just as our bodies need a balanced diet, our souls require a steady diet of Scripture. Our spirits cannot survive without the Word of God. God sets us a banquet. He offers us 31,173 nutrient-rich verses about himself and encourages us to feast! We nourish our hungry souls when we devote a balanced and generous amount of time to feasting on the truths of Scripture. It doesn't take long to notice the change. The Bible is life-giving — it revives every famished heart and breathes resurrection power into deathbed souls.

Discussion Questions:

1. Chapter three begins with two questions. Let's consider these. What if we do read the Bible everyday? What's supposed to happen?

2. Have you approached the Bible thinking that if it works for you, it will change your exterior circumstances rather than transforming your interior life so that your exterior circumstances are placed in their proper context?

3. What does it mean to have a life oriented to God?

4. Do you believe the Bible feeds or nourishes your spiritual life and soul?

5. If a healthy diet of high quality nutrients and a regular regimen of physical activity can completely transform your health and body what can a diet of Scripture do for your inner life?

6. In this chapter Brian talks about living from the inside out rather than the outside in. What does this mean to you?

7. What benefits and blessings would you hope for from a daily relationship with the Bible?

Reflection:

What challenged you in this chapter?

What will you do now? Based on today's discussion how specifically are you going to live this out this week?

Who will you tell? With whom will you have a spiritual conversation with about this weeks discussion?

Notes:

_____

_____

_____

_____

_____

_____

_____

_____

_____

_____

_____

_____

_____

_____

_____

_____

_____

_____

_____

_____

_____

_____

_____

CHAPTER FOUR
How The Bible Was Meant To Be Read

Read chapter four.

Summary:

Why is it so hard to read the Bible? I mean, we want to. We like the idea of it, but when we crack open the big book, we're lost. We have no real context for it, and randomly opening to a page and throwing down our finger hoping for a mystical revelation doesn't usually work well.

We feel like we must be failing as good Christians because we simply don't understand the Bible, and we can't find the time to figure out how to approach it. It's supposed to speak to us and guide us, but once we get beyond the verses we memorized in Sunday school, we're simply lost.

How do we actually get anything out of Bible study? If we're going to attempt an answer, we must put away the idea that the Bible is a rulebook we're supposed to measure up to or that it's so cryptic we need a Master of Theology degree to unlock it. Conversely, it's not a book full of dainty little promises from a God who more resembles Santa Claus than the Lord Almighty.

The Bible is a book about life. Our lives don't come to us in prepackaged bites, and neither does the Bible. Life comes at us in drama, intrigue, and emotion. Life comes to us as a story. We must approach the Bible as a story—the story of God and of God's people throughout history. What makes it dynamic and present today is that the story hasn't ended. We're each a part of the living, breathing story of God's passionate relationship with humankind, and we each have a place in it.

If we're going to grow into the maturity God has designed us to have, we must modify our thinking. We must begin to think in terms of wholeness, connection, and integration—about the proverbial forest as well as the trees. This is a stark contrast to modern culture, which has us parsing life into small, disconnected elements that we can arrange and rearrange to fit our circumstances. We experience this in the spiritual life when we divide biblical texts into sound bites rather than use the Bible as the baseline authority for life.

Think of it like this. Most of us desire nutrition that contains what our bodies need to remain healthy and vital. But the ideal is harder to achieve than the realities of life. Often we find ourselves settling for what we can get at a drive-thru because we've come unprepared to deal with what steals the day. Proper nutrition requires a complete commitment, and it requires the space in life that it takes to plan for and prepare these foods. In truth we have time for whatever we desire the most. If nutrition is nonnegotiable, it will be a reality in our lives. Spiritual nutrition works the exact same way.

The Bible was meant to be read in good-sized pieces. All of us probably know a variety of promises that the Scriptures offer. Plenty of verses comfort us when we're facing a struggle or encourage us as we take a risk. If we make these verses quaint, one-size-fits-all anecdotes for life's challenges, we'll be plagued by questions about why they don't always work. If we really desire to have the life Christ offers us, we must make reading Scripture in context—with space to breathe—a priority of our lives.

In order to have the relationship with Scripture that we sincerely desire, we must take a leap of faith and carve out time to breathe it in, to allow God's Word to speak to us. When we take this step, God will invariably show up.

Discussion Questions:

1. Have you ever randomly opened the Bible and thrown your finger down on a page hoping for God to speak to you?

2. Have you ever felt unsure about how to approach the Bible and find spiritual nourishment from it on your own?

3. Take a quick personal assessment of your spiritual life. Is your relationship with God largely about things you need or would like Him to do for you? If the honest answer is yes, how would that work if all your relationships were based on what the other person brought into your life rather than the give and take that long-term loving relationships require?

4. Based on your answer to the previous question what would you like to see change in your relationship with God?

5. In Chapter Four Brian says, "The Bible is a book about life. Our lives don't come to us in prepackaged bites, and neither does the Bible. Life comes at us in drama, intrigue, and emotion. Life comes to us as a story." Consider that the Bible is an unfolding story rather than a book of principles and regulations. Does that change your posture toward Scripture?

6. The Bible is meant to be read in context and often we find ourselves pulling a single verse to bring us comfort or encouragement. Have you ever gone to your favorite Scriptures and read them in their full context to understand why God said it the way He did? What did you discover?

7. Although most people would say that the Bible is something they can't quite find time for on a regular basis have you ever considered that perhaps it's the one thing you can't afford to live without? What would you have to move around in your life to allow for a spacious and breathing relationship with the Bible? What is keeping you from doing that? Why?

Reflection:

What challenged you in this chapter?

What will you do now? Based on today's discussion how specifically are you going to live this out this week?

Who will you tell? With whom will you have a spiritual conversation with about this weeks discussion?

Notes:

CHAPTER FIVE
Living The Bible In Community

Read chapter five.

Summary:

Too often we experience faith in a solitary way. We rarely think of it in terms of "us" and "our," and frequently see it as "me" and "my." But we can't mistake these Western, individualistic values for biblical values. The Bible is clear that living in community with other believers is irreplaceable in the Christian life.

The early church worshiped and lived communally. The Bible provides a detailed snapshot of what the church looked like at the beginning: "They devoted themselves to the apostles' teaching and to fellowship, to the breaking of bread and to prayer. Everyone was filled with awe at the many wonders and signs performed by the apostles. All the believers were together and had everything in common. They sold property and possessions to give to anyone who had need. Every day they continued to meet together in the temple courts. They broke bread in their homes and ate together with glad and sincere hearts, praising God and enjoying the favor of all the people. And the Lord added to their number daily those who were being saved" (Acts 2:42 – 47).

First Corinthians 12 says that we're all interconnected as the body of Christ, and so it's not possible to be free-standing, isolated entities. It's not possible to survive without each other. The bad news is that living in community requires sacrifice. The good news is that we can survive and thrive in community. The great news is that we have permission to be ourselves within community. We're uniquely placed. Our role is irreplaceable and our value immeasurable. A good many of the troubles that arise in community seem to come from our brokenness and insecurity, and so much of this happens because we ultimately think we're on our own and that we can survive that way.

We can't. When the body works together, there is enormous power to heal, restore, and renew what was sick and dying.

Once we understand with clarity that community is vital to our spiritual survival, we can begin to celebrate the beauty of how God has woven us together as one body and how important we are to each other's survival. Together we can participate in the abundant life Scripture describes; apart from each other we cannot. The Bible gives us our orientation to God and the baseline for living in community. It challenges our motivations and gives us the deep wisdom it takes to function as the body of Christ.

Christ is living in and through us (John 14:20; 17:23; Galatians 2:20; Colossians 1:27), and we, in community, are the hands and feet of Jesus in this world. As such we are commissioned and commanded to do the work of heaven on earth, and together, we have the incredible privilege of being participants in his kingdom coming and his will being done on earth as it is in heaven. This is how God has chosen to get his work in this world done.

What would happen to the world if we actually believed this? What would happen to the body of Christ if we believed it?

Discussion Questions:

1. Have you thought about the Bible in terms of "me" and "my" or "we" and "our?" Is the Bible only for personal reflection or is it meant to be something that guides a whole community of faith? What does that look like in your life?

2. Read 1 Corinthians 12. If we are a part of the same body why do we so often find ourselves trying to carve out our individuality in ways that isolate us?

3. What are the greatest challenges to living in community?

4. If everyone in your community committed to reading the Bible every day so that everyone was following the same rhythm of life what would be the result?

5. We've all heard the popular saying that we are, "the hands and feet of Jesus." What does this mean to you? Since hands and feet cannot do anything without the rest of the body how important is each person in your community to actually making a difference in your neighborhoods, churches and towns?

6. Read 1 Peter 5:8. Is this a metaphor or an actual reality?

7. If this is a reality are you more likely to withstand together or in isolation?

Reflection:

What challenged you in this chapter?

What will you do now? Based on today's discussion how specifically are you going to live this out this week?

Who will you tell? With whom will you have a spiritual conversation with about this weeks discussion?

Notes:

_____

_____

_____

_____

_____

_____

_____

_____

_____

_____

_____

_____

_____

_____

_____

_____

_____

_____

_____

_____

_____

_____

_____

CHAPTER SIX
Lectio Divina : Divine Reading

Read chapter six.

Summary:

Life isn't a race to the end but rather a gift given moment by moment. If we want to experience the abundant life God offers, we have to release our controlling, productivity-oriented approach to engaging faith and Scripture. So how do we give Scripture a spacious place to work in our lives? The answer lies in the ancient Christian practice of lectio divina.

In the early church of the 200s, some Christians chose to withdraw and seek God in the desert as a way of life. They lived an austere and simple existence, and it was in the desert that the ancient practice of lectio divina (Latin for "divine reading") began. Lectio divina is an unhurried, contemplative reading of a portion of Scripture, and it can give us a great framework for experiencing God through Scripture, meditation, prayer, and contemplation. Practicing lectio divina begins when we withdraw to a quiet or still place, with no agenda, checklist, or anticipated outlook in mind.

Lectio (read), the first step, is a slow reading of a brief passage of Scripture while listening for God to speak through it. We read it with a listening heart and invite God to speak to us through it. As we slowly read repeatedly, we look for any word or phrase that draws our attention. When we identify this word or phrase, we begin to meditate upon it.

Meditatio (mediation) is a time of quiet reflection in God's presence. Our goal is not to force ourselves into a mystical experience or even into deep insight, but to focus our affection and attention on God. We quietly read the words he's led us to in Scripture and slowly chew them. We interact with them, invite them to shed light on our thoughts and experiences, and permit God to connect these truths to our lives. Through this process we allow it to become his personal Word to us, speaking directly to our issues, decisions, hopes, and dreams—and his will for us in all of it.

The third step is oratio (prayer). We respond to what God has spoken to us through Scripture.

We often think of prayer as primarily talking to God, but what Scripture invites us to is conversational intimacy with God. We aren't coming to God with demands and petitions; rather, we're consecrating ourselves and asking that he take his Word into the deepest and most intimate places in our lives. We're inviting Christ into the places he's exposed or the moments he's taken us back to so that he might heal us and set us free (Luke 4:18).

Finally we enter into contemplatio, or contemplation, a time of rest. Here we entrust ourselves to God as we reflect on what he has spoken. We listen for any other words he may want to speak. We remain as still and close as friends or lovers who do not have the frantic need to fill the space with words. In contemplatio we come to a place of reverence and silence once again as we are released to fulfill God's purposes for us that day.

In practicing regular times of lectio divina, we not only allow the Holy Spirit to remind us of who we are and what our mission is; we also grow in intimacy with God. As this intimacy deepens, we become more like Christ.

Discussion Questions:

1. How has life felt like a losing race lately? How would your outlook change if you could receive life as a moment by moment gift?

2. Previous to this chapter had you ever heard of the ancient Christian practice of lectio divina?

3. The early Christians saw meditation on Scripture like a cow slowly chewing it's cud without distraction. What does that imagery bring up in your heart as you consider interacting with the Bible?

4. Let's talk about the four steps of lectio divina. The first is lectio. Choosing a portion of Scripture and allowing God to begin to draw our attention to what He'd like to say through simply reading slowly through it. Most people go to the Bible to get answers to something they are facing. Is it a new idea that we could go to the Bible to see what God might say rather than look for what we need Him to do?

5. The second step is meditatio. Quietly reflecting on what God is saying through Scripture we allow it to become His personal word to us. Often the process is one of trying to find the meaning with our intellect rather than simply allowing God to begin to speak to our hearts. Which way do you most often interact with Scripture? Through your intellect and reason or through your heart? What's the difference?

6. The third step is oratio. Contemplative prayer. Many people understand the idea of worship but they think it's largely done through music before a sermon. Most prayer lives are driven by our needs or on behalf of someone in need. Although these are certainly things God wants to hear have you ever thought about conversational intimacy with God? Have you ever had a time of prayer where you didn't set the tone or the agenda but rather simply made your heart present to whatever God might like to say to you? What was that like?

7. The final step in lectio divina is contemplation. Quiet contemplation. Simply being with God as with a truly trusted friend or spouse. The room doesn't need to be filled with words and there is no pressure to be anything but present. Have you ever tried spending time with God with no agenda?

Group Lectio Divina:

Choose a scripture and as a group move through the steps of lectio divina. You'll be surprised at what God will say to you through this beautiful time together in His presence.

Reflection:

What challenged you in this chapter?

What will you do now? Based on today's discussion how specifically are you going to live this out this week?

Who will you tell? With whom will you have a spiritual conversation with about this weeks discussion?

Notes:

_____

_____

_____

_____

_____

_____

_____

_____

_____

_____

_____

_____

_____

_____

_____

_____

_____

_____

_____

_____

_____

_____

_____

CHAPTER SEVEN
The Spoken Word, The Living Voice

Read chapter seven.

Summary:
Words spoken aloud are some of the most common but also most intriguing things in human experience. They form in our hearts and develop like film in the darkroom of our minds. We transfer them to our tongues, squeeze them by our cheeks, and slide them across our lips. They construct a living narrative and in the process set the tone and pace of life.

As the Bible developed over time and eventually transitioned from oral tradition to the written word, I have to wonder if something was lost. Is it possible that we now consider reading the Bible (silently) more important than experiencing the Bible as a spoken narrative, a living word? If so, what might we be missing?

Our interaction with Scripture can be expressed in many ways, and one of those ways is reading the Bible aloud. Scripture itself is full of instances that illustrate the power of what is spoken aloud, whether the words come from the mouth of God or the mouths of human beings. In Genesis 1, God speaks the world into existence. When Jesus announced his ministry and the reason he had come, he chose to do it while reading the Bible aloud (Luke 4). The gospel of John explains beautifully that the Word became flesh and made his dwelling among us in the person of Jesus (John 1:1 – 14). Hebrews 12 describes how the sound of God's voice shakes the earth and the heavens.

We could go on and on; the Bible demonstrates a clear precedent for interacting with the Word of God using our living voices (Proverbs 10:11; 18:21; Romans 10:9; 1 Thessalonians 4:18). So why do we generally choose to interact with the Bible only in silence?

I do not mean to diminish the power of the written word; in no way do I feel that quiet contemplation of the Word of God is a secondary approach to Scripture. But I do feel we are missing out if we limit our interaction with the Bible to silent reading. And I am convinced that the benefits of reading the Bible out loud and hearing it read aloud are more substantial than we realize.

I have read the Bible aloud in the company of others every day for over six years through the Daily Audio Bible, and the experience has changed my outlook on just about everything. I attribute these changes to the power of God's Word, but I believe firmly that the impact has been greatly magnified by reading it aloud. Speaking it myself and hearing it spoken by others makes God's Word something that has been declared as true rather than something yet to be considered and decided on.

I am utterly convinced that giving the Word of God a living voice is giving God a voice. These are his living words, the ones that tell the great story of God among us. As we speak them, we give them power in our lives. As your view of the Bible begins to transition from seeing it as a sacred object to embracing it as a beloved friend, give it voice. Read it aloud. Listen to it being read. Read it together with others.

If we give ear to the words of life, in the listening we will hear the voice of our heavenly Father as he speaks directly to our hearts.

Discussion Questions:

1. What is more powerful, a word that is thought or a word that is spoken? Why?

2. Have you always thought that the Bible was something to pore over only in quiet contemplation rather than something that can also be spoken aloud?

3. Have you ever considered that the Word of God spoken aloud becomes the spoken Word of God as if God were speaking directly to you out loud?

4. There are times in the life of a believer that we cry out to God to speak and give us clarity and direction. Have you considered reading aloud from God's Word as a way to hear Him speak clearly to you?

5. Read John 10:9-15 silently. Now choose someone to read it aloud. Was there a difference in what you heard or absorbed by hearing the words of Jesus spoken aloud?

Reflection:

What challenged you in this chapter?

What will you do now? Based on today's discussion how specifically are you going to live this out this week?

Who will you tell? With whom will you have a spiritual conversation with about this weeks discussion?

Notes:

_____

_____

_____

_____

_____

_____

_____

_____

_____

_____

_____

_____

_____

_____

_____

_____

_____

_____

_____

_____

_____

_____

CHAPTER EIGHT
Living The Bible In Your Family

Read chapter eight.

Summary:

I have no doubt that you, like me, love your kids. And I have no doubt that you, like me, often worry about our children's spiritual lives. We know that we can't coerce our children into an intimate relationship with Jesus; it won't happen by default. But we do want them to understand the importance of a relationship with Jesus and a life lived in fellowship with him.

The book of Exodus shows us that the effect we have on our children is profound, that the choices we make and the posture of our lives matter greatly both to us and to our kids. The children of Israel learned this lesson in a sobering way, and the next generation paid the price by not being able to enter the Promised Land, as God had intended for them to do. (You can read the whole story in the book of Exodus.)

There are parallels between this story and the state of the world today that should tug at our hearts and possibly bring us to our knees. We, like the Israelites, find ourselves bowing the knee to false gods that pull our hearts away from God. When we grumble and complain about what we do not have and cannot get to a place of trusting satisfaction in God, the longer it takes for us to arrive at a place of freedom in Christ, and the more we force our children to wander along with us.

As parents, we fail much of the time, but our falling short is not an indictment, judgment, or sentence—it's a wake-up call. It's a line in the sand. If we want our kids to learn to honor, love, and accept Jesus as Savior, we have to model it for them. If we actually want the Christian life to be abundant in our families, we will have to develop an intimacy with Scripture ourselves.

There is time and there is grace. It doesn't matter where you are now; there is always an opportunity to commit to a God-honoring path for your family. Will you begin now?

Discussion Questions:

1. In the past how have you intentionally tried to introduce your kids to the Bible?

2. Brian says in this chapter that no matter how slick the resource and no matter how hard we try none of it will convince our kids IF we're not actually living the example of our faith and devotion to the Bible in our own lives. Is this true?

3. If our children assume (in their youth) that the way we do things as parents is the "right way," what is the message of our lives sending as it relates to our relationship with God and His Word?

4. In this chapter the example of the Children of Israel denying their faith in God on the very verge of entering the Promised Land and thereby dooming an entire generation of children to grow up wandering in the desert when they were destined to be raised in a land flowing with milk and honey is offered. It was the children who had to grow up and complete the job their parents had failed to do. Had you ever noticed this in Scripture before? How can we, as parents, not repeat this same story?

Prayer:

Chapter eight concludes with a prayer. Pray this together and enter into a personal time of prayer alone or if you are studying together as a group over your families and children.

Heavenly Father, It is our deepest desire to introduce our children and our entire families to the truth of your Word. More importantly, it is our heart's desire to fling open the doors and windows of our homes to you. We know this begins with us.

Come, Holy Spirit. We invite you into the attics and corners, the closets and basements of our very souls. Nothing is off limits to you. We invite you to shine the light of truth into every area of our lives. Create in us a clean heart and renew a right spirit within us that we may serve you well. Guide us in the coming days so we can introduce our children to your ways and show them what a true relationship with you looks like. Help us to create a passion for your Word in our families by having such a passion in our own hearts.

By the authority of the work of Jesus we now take authority in our homes and reject anything there that does not honor you. We commit our children to you. We commit our relationships to you. We bow to your authority by giving you your rightful place at the center of our lives. This we pray in the mighty and victorious name of Jesus our Savior. Amen.

Reflection:

What challenged you in this chapter?

What will you do now? Based on today's discussion how specifically are you going to live this out this week?

Who will you tell? With whom will you have a spiritual conversation with about this weeks discussion?

Notes:

_____

_____

_____

_____

_____

_____

_____

_____

_____

_____

_____

_____

_____

_____

_____

_____

_____

_____

_____

_____

_____

_____

CHAPTER NINE
Finding Your Place In God's Story

Read chapter nine.

Summary:

  Once I took a ride south along Highway 1 in Oregon along the Pacific Ocean. When I came across a massive stretch of empty beach, I hiked down the sand embankment in the rain to the coast. A few more paces down the coastal prairie path and I was on the open beach, walled in by massive rock formations rising from the ocean floor that captured and amplified her roar. I was overcome by the sheer power of the waves. I felt like a speck, like one of the grains of sand.

  Facing the roar of the open sea, I had to bow to the creative force of God, who first conceived it and then spoke it into existence — a mere symbol of his glory and power. Unexpectedly a wave of heartache washed over me with the thought of my children, who were growing faster than I was comfortable with. It wasn't the kind of heartache that left me hopeless; it was the kind that any parent can relate to. We are caretakers for but a moment, and then we hold our breath, cross our fingers, and breathe a fervent prayer as we watch them float away to write their own chapters on the tablets of history.

  This is the kind of longing and profound love our heavenly Father feels for us. He creates a world for us, new every day, perhaps holding his breath and hoping to draw us closer to his heart. He leads and guides, but when all is said and done, we each choose freely where we will go.

  I have denied God in my life. I've questioned every value I was ever taught. I've resented. I've run. But time has allowed me to see that I was blaming God for everything I ever saw go wrong, heaping on him everything I could not explain on my own. It took years to realize that God wasn't behaving questionably. People were. I was.

And God was watching the whole time, sending me love notes in a sunset or in an unexpected snow covering the Tennessee hill country. I would have never understood this without the Bible. Never.

Finding your place in God's story means listening with the ears of your heart and living life in the poetic rather than the purely rational. To find enrichment from Scripture while participating in an authentic relationship with God, we must reclaim the aspect of our faith that encourages a state of wonder, or a more poetic experience of faith. We can't force the deepest of spiritual matters to submit to the will of reason without doing violence to them; this is not how faith operates.

The writer of Hebrews declares, "Faith is confidence in what we hope for and assurance about what we do not see" (Hebrews 11:1). Faith includes more than the rational mind alone can perceive. In order to locate ourselves in God's story, we have to place reason in its proper position and give faith its rightful place. We have to look at the world through the eyes of the poet by embracing more than reason. We must be open to things like art to capture and express what is otherwise inarticulate about our experience of God. This is where God resides.

Why won't God speak more clearly to us? we wonder. Oh, but he is. He is always speaking to us, through everything, everywhere — and he's given us this book, telling us the story of who we are and the enormous lengths he's been willing to go through to bring us back home. Slow down and look around you. God is calling your name.

Discussion Questions:

1. Had you ever considered that the loving heart of the Heavenly Father is that of any parent as they hope and long for the best for their children? Do you see yourself as a child of God?

2. Have you ever blamed God for not showing up to rescue you from something you got yourself into? Why do we do this?

3. Do you believe God wants to speak to you? Do you believe He gave us the Bible as a way to speak undeniably as a loving Father into our lives each day? If so, does this make you long to hear what He has to say?

4. What does it mean to listen with the ears of your heart?

5. In chapter nine Brian says, "Why won't God speak more clearly to us? we wonder. Oh, but he is. He is always speaking to us, through everything, everywhere—and he's given us this book, telling us the story of who we are and the enormous lengths he's been willing to go through to bring us back home. Slow down and look around you. God is calling your name." Does this change your perception of what the Bible is to us?

Reflection:

What challenged you in this chapter?

What will you do now? Based on today's discussion how specifically are you going to live this out this week?

Who will you tell? With whom will you have a spiritual conversation with about this weeks discussion?

Notes:

_____

_____

_____

_____

_____

_____

_____

_____

_____

_____

_____

_____

_____

_____

_____

_____

_____

_____

_____

_____

_____

_____

CHAPTER TEN
No Joke, You Will Never Be The Same

Read chapter ten.

Summary:

There is nothing that I believe will create the change we want to see in the world more than if God's people will read God's Word every day and be transformed by the power contained within it. Reading the Bible has changed me, and it can do the same for you. This is a promise. If you read the Bible every day for a year, you will not be the same. Immersing yourself in the truth of God's Word will make you different and change your life. So what are you waiting for?

You won't be the same after truly encountering the Bible. You won't care about some of the things you care a lot about now. Some of the things that seem huge in life at the moment are going to simply not matter this time next year. It's true that the stresses and distractions of life will be forced into their proper perspective, but the Bible will never offer the comfort of complacency. It will never allow stagnation. It will never allow us to depend on ourselves and create alternative plans that get things done without God anymore. That isn't life.

The Bible is about becoming more like Christ. It constantly invites us to submit ourselves in obedience not to make us miserable but to change us from the inside out. An authentic relationship with Jesus is an all-or-nothing proposition, and this requires change. Some changes will likely come hard — it's not easy to untangle all the kudzu that's been growing around our hearts and minds as we've done our best to make life work on our own terms. It's not particularly pleasant to allow the Holy Spirit to move into the wounded places in our lives and begin to truly heal what has been oozing bitterness and disappointment. None of this comes easily, but you don't have to do it alone. God's Word is the friend you have needed all along, and in co-operation with the Holy Spirit (John 16:7), you will never walk alone (Matthew 28:20).

Go look in the mirror. Look deeply into your eyes. After journeying through the Bible every day for a year, I'd love for you to return to the mirror. You're likely to see new life twinkling from behind those eyes that isn't there right now. Those stresses and worries that are pulling at you aren't going to be the giants they can seem to be these days. You're going to be different. You will have been transformed from the inside out, but you won't likely get there by any of the roads you've ever traveled before. This is the beauty of being in love, and this is the adventure of traveling with one who knows where all the hidden and breathtaking vistas are.

May you find life in God's Word, my friend, and may true life find you.

Discussion Questions:

1. If all of God's people spent time each day being fed from God's Word what would happen to the world? Would the change we long for begin to take place? Is there any reason this shouldn't start right here in your life or in this group?

2. If Jesus were to ask you to let him heal your broken heart but that meant you had to let him take you to the places that are broken would you let him? What does that thought bring up inside you?

4. After going through this whole book do you now long for the kind of change that Scripture offers even if that means letting go of some of things that are comfortable but that may be killing you inside?

5. Has Passages given you a new desire to fall in love with the Bible? Could it be the best friend you've never had?

Reflection:

What challenged you in this chapter?

What will you do now? Based on today's discussion how specifically are you going to live this out this week?

Who will you tell? With whom will you have a spiritual conversation with about this weeks discussion?

Notes:

_____

_____

_____

_____

_____

_____

_____

_____

_____

_____

_____

_____

_____

_____

_____

_____

_____

_____

_____

_____

_____

Conclusion

It's my deepest prayer that as you complete your journey through Passages: How Reading The Bible In A Year Will Change Everything For You that another journey has begun; your personal journey through the Bible in a year and beyond. I pray that the Bible becomes a trusted friend that walks with you every day for the rest of your life.

The Daily Audio Bible may be an indespensible resource in walking with you. Go to www.dailyaudiobible.com for more information. I look forward to our adventure together through the Bible. It's unbelievable what can happen in a year.

Blessings,
Brian